# VOCATION

POEMS

Ken Autrey

DOS MADRES

2025

# DOS MADRES PRESS INC.
P.O. Box 294, Loveland, Ohio 45140
www.dosmadres.com    editor@dosmadres.com

Dos Madres is dedicated to the belief that the small press is essential
to the vitality of contemporary literature as a carrier of the new voice,
as well as the older, sometimes forgotten voices of the past. And in an
ever more virtual world, to the creation of fine books pleasing to the
eye and hand.

Dos Madres is named in honor of Vera Murphy and Libbie Hughes,
the "Dos Madres" whose contributions have made this press possible.

Dos Madres Press, Inc. is an Ohio Not For Profit Corporation and a
501 (c) (3) qualified public charity. Contributions are tax deductible.

Executive Editor: Robert J. Murphy

Illustration & Book Design: Elizabeth H. Murphy
www.illusionstudios.net

Typeset in Adobe Garamond Pro & New York
ISBN 978-1-962847-30-8
Library of Congress Control Number: 2025942323

*For my teachers, students,*
*and companions in poetry,*
*all of whom continue to inspire me*

# TABLE OF CONTENTS

## THE VOICES

Voices at Mid-Cut ........................................................1
Imagining Iowa, January 1936 ...............................2
Half-Truths ................................................................4
Grandfather................................................................5
Foremother ................................................................6
First Watch.................................................................7
Fishing Deep ..............................................................8
Barn on Sand Hill ......................................................9
Embers......................................................................12
Old Stone..................................................................13
The Workshop...........................................................15
Plumbers...................................................................17
Resurrection .............................................................19

## THE CALLINGS

Saint Joan in the Garden .........................................23
Writer........................................................................24
Denim Quilt .............................................................25
Man with a Red Hat .................................................26
Cutouts.....................................................................28
The Poet Moves to Chicago ......................................30
The Poet Meets His Class in the Chemistry Lab ........31
The Surgeon at Night ...............................................33
Altar..........................................................................35
Dispatcher.................................................................36
The Photographer......................................................37
Yogi...........................................................................38
Bruja .........................................................................40
Biosphere 2 ...............................................................42
Policeman..................................................................43
Transients..................................................................44

# THE WORK

Logjam ...................................................47

First Grade Teacher ................................48

Mrs. Perry ............................................49

Coach...................................................51

Haircut.................................................52

Day Shift..............................................54

Microscope...........................................55

Bamboo................................................57

Gold Country ......................................59

Culture.................................................61

Bat in the House ..................................63

Fruition................................................65

One Mug at a Time..............................66

Sawhorse ..............................................67

The Dream of Teaching .......................68

The Butterfly Tattoo ............................69

The Student Poets.................................70

Volcano ................................................71

Flare .....................................................72

Drawing................................................73

# THE PATH

Postcards ..............................................77

Sanctuary .............................................78

Finding Mexico ....................................79

Machu Picchu ......................................80

Olives...................................................81

Laundry ...............................................83

Good Friday .........................................84

In Manila .............................................85

Outpost.................................................87

The Letters ...........................................88

National Geographic ..................................................90
Dry Season in Ghana ...............................................91
Hard Bargain...........................................................93


About the Author....................................................95
Acknowledgements...................................................96

VOCATION

THE VOICES

# Voices at Mid-Cut

You are repairing the porch,
a job that's needed doing
since before your parents'
last visit.  Sawhorses firmly set,
you hitch your carpenter's apron,
score the wood with a pencil,
rev the circular saw, and bite
into the line, knee and palm
steadying the one-inch board.
Over the blade's whine you hear
your mother's voice, stopping
the saw at mid-cut (something
your father told you
never to do) and wait.

A sliver bothers the knuckle
of your index finger.
You could use your mother's help
with that, her gleaming tweezers
tilted like a surgeon's tool,
but you cannot hear a word.
You square the saw, notice
a little gouge you did not want,
and start her up, this time
cutting to the end, left hand
reaching just in time to catch
the remnant board.  You think
just as the saw dies down
your father's hands ought to be
the ones you turn to in the heat
of outdoor work, his voice the sound
that calls you to your task.

# Imagining Iowa, January 1936

Cows breathe clouds
into the snow-piled lot
behind the college barn,
trusting my father's arrival.
At 5 a.m., black boots on numb feet,
he slides open the door enough
to admit the herd single file.
The Jerseys enter a sweet gloom
and sway into stanchions,
where there's a scoop of grain
for each frosted muzzle.

Three hours before chemistry class,
drained from late study, one hand
curls the first cow's flyswatter tail
onto her bony hips.  With his other,
he dips a towel into hot water
to bathe the bulging udder,
thumb-sized nipples pink
and wrinkled.  Then,
he positions the steel milk can,
suction of its tubes driven
by a distant electric wheezing.

His hands, raw in Iowa's unrelenting winter,
are soothed by the chlorine-rich water,
heartbeat of machines lulling
him into shallow sleep as sunrise
colors the air.  The cows yield
their milk in the bone-deep cold,
as he drifts through an aching

dream that feeds his hunger
for the gentle hills of Louisiana
or some way of going on
as faithfully as the maternal cows.

## Half-truths

Snapshots in the tattered album
blur my parents' tale. When I free
a photo from its arrowhead corners,
the one of her leaning on a shiny car
with a strange man, I flip it over,
finding nothing on its back.
In another, my father,
in the dark overcoat and felt hat
every man wore in the thirties,
drapes his arm around a blonde,
faintly labeled "Anita." Then she's gone
in the next frame. Light cast
on the pages deepens the shadows.

I'll settle for half-truths, just enough
of the past to fuel my own flawed memories:
a woman glimpsed in the trees across
a languid stream, the pickup rumbling
through midnight, its driver now faceless,
dignitaries in the funeral procession,
me on tip toe to see it all,
surrounded by strangers, some weeping.

# Grandfather

Midsummer.  Only bony ends
of an old man's life lean
from a hospital window in Shreveport.
He shuns the light green gowns,
insists on undershirts showing
wing-like shoulders.  Nearly gone--
lungs that huffed through a life
breathing oil field fumes
and manure-scented hay dust.

One wave down to me--all I have
from the man who told everyone,
"Never break for lunch until you reach
the end of a row."  The old ones say
his actions said it all: his fidgety
hands, his one-arm pushups, his felling
each tree with precision.  In the one
photo: fresh-pressed khaki,
the background fig tree,
a slight smile on his angular face.

Now, too far gone to take the cure,
he stands, immobile for once
in Louisiana, framed by the highest
window he ever looked through.

# Foremother

The grandmother I never knew,
gone in my mother's thirteenth year,
painted China. She left
saucers, cups, and dishes
with gilt edges and flourishes,
tiny yellow roses, perfect
in their haloes of green.

Her initials loop
in ornate whorls.
Grasping this pitcher's
cool surface as she did,
I feel how soft fingers
in time blurred the gold
edging the fragile handle.

Cradling the work
she wrought,
I want to claim
part of her--
unsullied hands,
white as the porcelain she gilded,
wrists supple as her monogram.

It's delicate, this calling
back to life a woman I know
so little of, who makes up
one-fourth of me. I have only
faint photos to help me,
those and the fading
lines of her steady brush.

# First Watch

Seasons you waited at sea
hearing your watch tick.
Now that it's mine I'm your son,
scanning the circle of numbers,
hoping for signs, hands going round.

I hardly need to know the time.
Still, I wind it up,
listen to the cadence
echoing your months from home.
What does the salt tick tell?

You wore it when your ship sailed east,
out of the moon blown New York harbor,
and signal lights blinked news of my birth.
Months through midnight sentries,
fogs, ragged ports after war:

What ship escaped us in that first long year
as I unfolded in Mother's care?
Back home you struggled
to find your land legs, your fatherhood.
I never saw you wear the watch.

Years later you gave it to me.
I used it a year or two, took it off,
put it with knives and coins.
I keep the watch in my drawer
where your granddaughter's fingers delve.

When she knows about waiting
I'll give it to her.

## Fishing Deep

Lately even our luck
with crickets has failed.
On the freshwater, my father
and I have taken to chatting
about the sunrise or the taunting
cry of the fish crow.
When we've surprised ourselves
and caught a few,
they've been small throwbacks.

It's time to return
to fishing deep. The gear alone
can break you, and choppy seas
threaten, but Dad, a Navy man,
could choose the weekend and bargain
with the captain. We could try
the Gulf as we did once
or twice in the old days.

It should come back to me:
how you work by feel,
instead of the silly bounce
of a plastic cork, how you surrender
the bait deeply in hope
of some large return, how leaning
toward the unsteady sea you trust
your hands to know when to leave
well enough alone, when to set
the hook, and when to pull
for all you're worth.

# Barn on Sand Hill

## I.

The barn on my father's farm tilts
between chinaberry trees.
Only fire could collapse it,
never the burden of cotton
baled long before my day,
nor restless sheep thronging
through tottering doors,
nor weedy years of no crops.

The barn planks whorl like smoke,
old as the cotton-leached land.
Still wisps of fiber cling
to the hewn rafters and twist
in rolls of barbed wire
as they did when I sat in hay
mending the tattered bridle,
soaping the saddle at dusk.

The square lot beside the barn
opens out onto fields.
It's where the burro kicked
at the dogs in dust of August,
and Herefords lowly whined,
orange flanks lodged at the trough.
Sparrows pecked the leavings
when the herd turned to pasture.

When I see the fence stretch out,
post after black post,
My fingers stiffen as if gloved.
Reels of wire pulled at me
as we worked the fence each September,
south to the hickory grove,
north to the county road.
We rested in sassafras shade.

II.

Albert lost his way into the barn
one spring just as trees came out green.
His hair flared like fire, and he slept
in the hay with a cotton blanket
as wind whipped over the rafters.
By day he would squat in sunlight,
arms crooked on his knees, rubbing
his back on a rough fence rail.

In patched and baggy shorts,
a fading flowered shirt,
Albert would walk up the hill,
tamping his corncob pipe,
to smoke until the sun settled.
Crouching close to the earth and silent,
perhaps he was watching for deer
or hawks curling into the night.

Once drawn to a broken tractor,
he unlocked the gears, leaving
them splayed on burlap, oiled
in glistening geometry.
We discovered Albert one morning;
the blanket lay over him still,
his vision widely lost
in the barn's ribbed recesses.

Now the sun spills over the trees
as I walk the discernible path
through half-open, chain-laden gates
and come into an animal realm,
turning back to the place
where the withering pasture subsides,
the lot closes over in pokeweed,
and the barn stands lively and dark.

# Embers

Dad's fires in the backyard pit
started wild, shrunk to a murmur,
then turned to charcoal embers
that lasted the evening.
Gusts of wind blew sparks up,
brought the coals to fleeting life.
before they subsided.

The next morning, I rushed out
to hold a palm over the coals,
test their warmth, and stir them
with a stick, peering for
a lingering glow. I cast a handful
of dry leaves onto the ashes,
hoping they'd flare up.

When I weed the garden, repair
the roof, paint a table, my limbs
on a good day warm to the task,
fade into my father's frame, take on
his wrinkles. What never ages—
this working to revive
the heat of his life, my life.

## Old Stone

The stone with its indentation,
oddly symmetrical, surfaced
in the back yard when I was young.
The size of a half-deflated basketball,
weighing maybe twelve pounds,
it sat years on the verge
of a flower bed Dad nurtured,
then neglected. Later it lay
under azaleas. I gave it no more
thought than anything else.
Fifty years gone, I come home
to the old house, and one day,
wandering near the blueberry patch
nearly trip over the worn relic
I'd forgotten and now see
with aging eyes as one remnant
of a settlement on this hill long before
the plantation orchard that predated
our neighborhood but lingers
as several ragged pecan trees.
An archaeologist tells me
it's a nutting stone, cupped surface
for crushing, socket for holding
a spear shaft while bark peeling,
seat for a fire-making bow drill,
or mortar for grinding pigments
and medicinal herbs. This remnant
of a culture sits now in our bird bath,
perch for cardinal and finch
as they sip, then scan the lawn.

It's a compact altar, emblem of a world
that couldn't endure, trapped now
in our transient moment, resting where
on warm evenings we kids played croquet,
then put down our mallets to sit among
the wickets as Dad pulled up a lawn chair to tell
stories of a lost childhood, long months at sea,
migration to this patient land where
Creek potsherds pepper the landscape
and the turning earth awaits our passage.

# The Workshop

I've spent the afternoon in the workshop
my father built a good fifty years back
on a hill outside of town. Today I've
driven here in my pickup not to build
a set of shelves, plane a new leaf
for the dining room table, or refinish
a ladderback chair. This time I give
myself over to sorting the jumble
of nails, bolts, washers, fasteners,
hinges, and screws he left behind.

In the end the care that once led him
to hang every wrench in its place
and drop every unused nut
in the assigned plastic drawer,
gave way to the entropy of dementia,
the chaos inside him spilling over
into the dust and gloom of this home
away from home that even sunlight
through the huge plate glass windows
could not dispel.

I am following his footsteps
back and forth across the plank floor
as I breathe in the fumes of oil and oak
that sustained him even after he lost
the craftsman's know-how that came
from a depression- plagued farm
in Louisiana. Sifting through shards
and remnants he left behind,
much of it rusted and useless,
I'm after something more than order.

I'm finally old enough, just
a few years short of the age he died,
to know that setting things right is more
than getting all the 10-penny nails
in one Maxwell House coffee can, more
than sequencing all the drill bits by size.
Maybe one day I too will lose my bearings,
haunt the places I love without recalling
what first drew me to them. Others,
perhaps my daughters, may one day
make sense of my late wandering
in some cluttered room or patch of woods
and somehow rediscover my voice, my touch.

# Plumbers

My mother calls to say
the plumbers are replacing
corroded pipes in the house
where I grew up. She's in bed
cradling the phone
with large numbers
I installed last year.

Two men work under her house
in the crawl space. They promise
they'll use only copper.
I hear the muffled clatter
of a wrench on pipes so clogged
it's been impossible
to take a shower.

I wish I were there
to inspect their work, but what
do I know about plumbing?
What do I know about
my mother, whose days
unroll like bandages, one
spliced into the next?

She surrounds herself with clippings
from magazines she stacks in the corner.
Sometimes she reads one to me--
a new way to stop heart disease
or an idea for preserving old photos,
though at my age I'm less concerned
with preservation than what to throw away.

Her youth in the depression
and her mother's early death
make her want to keep everything.
She says she'll have them save one pipe
that's like a sick artery, so clogged
she holds it like a telescope
and can't see through it.

# Resurrection

In afterlife, they say, the hair grows on.
Bones find their level; strands engulf the grave,
unearthly cavern holding its icon
of black curl, of Madonna's yearning wave.
The undertaker's shovel, parson's tome,
the widow's tears, one scarlet outlaw rose:
all four converge to give the hair its home
away from home, its cringing at repose.
The body's fires may cool, its flesh defiled.
But after all, they say, the hair grows wild.

# THE CALLINGS

# Saint Joan in the Garden

—after Jules Bastien-Lepage's painting, *Jeanne d'Arc*

I imagined you in armor, only
your smooth face giving away
your femininity, or bound
to the stake burning placidly,
after your fortunes turned, after
going on with the tattered banner.

But here I find you in
your parents' cluttered garden,
leaning out of an earlier life
where you were only a woman
in bare feet with weaving to do.

Two imploring saints hover
transparently behind you,
above an overturned chair,
an abandoned loom. Your startled
face shows that quaint furniture
has already fallen into the past.

Your left arm stretches forward
as if something unseen
coaxes you away. In the burning
eyes and clenched right fist,
the way your bodice is working
loose, I find a woman ready
to strip away her womanhood
yearning to wear the armor,
beginning the other story.

# Writer

—after Milton Avery's painting, *Girl Writing*

The girl with neither name nor face
sits on a wooden stool, legs pretzeled
together above pink socks. Her left hand
splays on a plain desk top suspended
before a dark wall and grips a pen
as delicate as a thorn, touching it
to a blur of notepaper edged in pink.
Her forehead rests on her right fist,
elbow propped on the writing surface.
Dense black hair drops to her shoulders,
the contrast with the white brushstrokes
of her dress almost too stark. Plenty
about this study forces itself
upon us; plenty too stays obscure:
her message, the story
of her muscular body, each
as secret as the other. Where
did they send him? We make do
with the fine needlework
on one puffed sleeve and the nearly
invisible spray of blossoms perfuming
the air, pulling her back to some
recent afternoon that slipped away.

# Denim Quilt

—after Lutisha Pettway's quilt, *Bars*

Nine strips worn from work, torn
from overalls, sun-faded and patched,
unadorned by anything but dark
pocket marks showing where once
a kerchief lodged in heat, lay
sweat-saturated, timeless, until
my final stitch at one corner and then
a scrub with lye soap, immersion
in a kettle of hot water, and drying
under the same sun that bleached
the denim and wrung out my man.

Then falls evening when such
a cover showing all the ancient blues
of sky's reprisals, rests like a blessing
on our hand-hewn bed, us stretched
beneath remains of ragged britches
dragged through cotton and corn,
once rough protection from all
that forced us here, leaving us
with little but threadbare hope
that this faint square will serve
as anything but a shroud.

# Man with a Red Hat

—after Jerry Siegel's photograph, *Can Man*

A thin man,
white trousers rolled
above bony knees,
wears dress shoes
and dark socks,
white shirt buttoned
over a black one
with tails loose.
A cardboard box
of crushed cans
hangs from
his flexed left arm
like a battered suitcase.
His limbs are thin as
the distant phone poles.
A muted sky,
the blur of trees,
the road angling away:
all fade back from
the bright cans and
a watch band shining.
He might have just
stepped off a bus,
fumes still hanging
in the gray air.
Or he's waiting for
the next one into town
to redeem his aluminum
bounty gleaned from

miles of shoulder,
his lonely roadside
sojourn lit only
by scant sun
and a porkpie hat
red as Christmas,
flat beacon
glowing through mist.

# Cutouts

Shirt pocket bulging with paper squares
he slides out a purple sheet, folds it
to make an accordion.
                    From his trousers
he pulls a Swiss Army knife and snaps
open the scissors. His fingers shift
and swivel, snipping
                    away shards,
triangles, fingernails of scrap. Cuts
and gaps soon riddle the narrow slab.
He folds the blades
                    back into their furrow,
tucks away the knife, and opens
the bunched paper like a package.
Now the cutout
                    spreads into
a star, a heart, an arrow,
a bowlegged cowboy. All
unfurl to life on
                    one four-inch plane
his nimble fingers smooth out.
The old hands came to muscle
in the town mill
                    where he started
as lapper in the picker room and soon
began to work the drawing frame,
feeding fiber through
                    as slivers.
In time he worked his way up, becoming
doffer, spinner, spooler and then overseer
of the weaving line

where warp and weft,
beam and harness, guided those days now gone
to mills abroad, where alien hands wind and creel
the endless thread in hot rooms.

# The Poet Moves to Chicago

—for David Starkey

He knows if he can write a villanelle
he's smart enough to move his wife
and kids to Chicago.  The rented van
is crammed, discards piled on the curb
like broken lines that wouldn't scan.
Now it's just the two lawn chairs
he's bound to find room for in the snarl
of bicycles and bed frames roped
into place.  The kids are wandering
about the empty house, looking teary
and disoriented.  His wife's face
is beet red.  He's tempted to chuck
the flimsy chairs into the pile
of debris, but then how fine
it will be when all is settled
and he can snap one of these
into place beside the pool,
sip a good local beer, and read works
of the Chicago writers.  Some things
you can't compromise on--the heft
of a well-turned metaphor, say, or
the vision of a truck laden
with everything that matters.

# The Poet Meets His Class in the Chemistry Lab

The periodic chart is God here,
benign beginnings of everything
above the white-scrawled
blackboard, gas nozzles,
fierce arcing faucets,
acid-stained sinks.

The place dazzles with glass--
beakers, tubes, flasks,
and pipettes. Their very names
exude sulfurous fumes.
"Don't break anything,"
the poet says and bangs his briefcase
on the black lab table.

"Nothing's sacred here.
Alchemy lives," he proclaims
and fires up a bunsen burner,
pulling cork-stoppered jars
from the shelves.
Apprentices fidget
on wooden stools. He mutters,
"Let's cook some poems."

Students push books aside
in the spirit of science.
They mix white powders
and golden liquids like so many
metaphors, improvising rhythms
in the spit and pop of the moment.

They are cast into their mothers'
kitchens again to concoct sauces
and dare each other to taste them.

## The Surgeon at Night

Strolling from the dark garden,
where chrysanthemums thrive,
the surgeon inspects his house
like peeping Tom.  Through one window
he sees a kitchen sink laden with dishes,
utensils strewn on counters.
The world is cold as an operating room.
His sighs bring steam into air,
tracings that melt like the blink
of the year's third snowflake.
Opaque feet in the rimed grass
anchor him under a sterile sky.
The surgeon's work was completed
by mid-afternoon.  Now, bright scalpels
only a recollection, his fingers turn numb.
The day, like a trunk of bandages, slips
over the border.  No movement blurs
the rooms he views, still lives behind glass.
Could he lift these bright tableaus
and hang them on other houses
or pack them for viewing in a distant city?
In the dwindling yard, the surgeon takes
from his coat pocket a white cotton mask.
Bandit-like, he ties it on his chilly face,
crimping the metal wire at the bridge
of his nose.  He looks for some flicker
of life inside the warm house.  Then
a light winks off in the den,
on in an upstairs bedroom.  He hears
the whine of a neighbor's dog,

asking to go inside.  Later,
when the surgeon climbs beneath the drapes
of his bed and feels the pulse
in his wife's slender neck, he will recall
how the cold sharpens all things and clarifies
the air, allowing light from stars
to drop unimpeded into his own yard.

# Altar

The bride in her pastel
kitchen keeps her crystal out,
polishes silver at noon, racks
all knives symmetrically
and misses her mother's
flour-dusted cupboards.
On the formica counter--
a bruise of spilt coffee,
a thin ribbon of milk.
This is the start
of new reason: gentle
breakage, tarnished vow,
blade of doubt.

## Dispatcher

Through a life in Pennsylvania
coal country, his black hair,
wet anthracite parted neatly,
never grayed. Wire-rim glasses,
a sharp nose, a broad smile—
he could have been
a slick banker in a white shirt
but worked the trains,
tapping Morse code with large hands
until the Scranton line closed.
At 60, too young to retire,
he took a job making fish sticks,
baking them to perfection
in massive ovens, laying them
like rail ties in heavy pans.
When the Susquehanna flooded
his two-story house on Cherry Street,
the old photos were ruined,
but until death he told stories
in a constant chuckle:
the mine collapse, his Boy Scout
misadventures, the fools
he worked with, the sound
of fading train whistles.

# The Photographer

lips a cigar as he studies
a two-dimensional version
of himself, white shirt, arms
akimbo. Now, he's an old man
with a gray beard in a flannel shirt.
A puff of smoke blurs the figure
staring at him from thirty years back.
He's frozen in the past. Not even
the full box of safety matches
on the table could burn away
the years, restore the knobby fingers
to their smooth, pliant beginnings.

But now the smoker is not sure
it's his younger self at all.
He doesn't recognize the high,
gleaming forehead, the slight smirk,
or the weathered plank backdrop.
Is this merely one in the parade
of characters he posed and peered at
through a lens, through the years?
Is there a name penciled on the back?

Of late, he's not picked up
a camera, has all but lost the feel
of the sturdy lens in his left palm,
the sound of a moment snapping
free of its moorings, the eye-watering
smell of developer solution,
the thrill of watching a face
clarify and rise through amber liquid.

# Yogi

*A yogi engages in a definite, step-by-step procedure by which the body and mind are disciplined, and the soul liberated. Taking nothing for granted on emotional grounds, or by faith, a yogi practices a thoroughly tested series of exercises which were first mapped out by the early sages.*

—Paramhansa Yogananda

Back straight, legs tucked
neatly under him, he wears
a white robe, has unkempt hair
and a gray beard,
He sits and meditates
when not contorting his body
or posing immobile like a stork
one-legged at the edge of a swamp.
He perches on a remote cliff
or in a cavernous shrine,
eyes half-closed, expressionless.

If he has followers, they are silent,
trembling in their obeisance.
They await his terse commands,
revere his unwavering freedom
from hunger, anxiety, everything.

Rows of women
in black tights unroll their mats
in lofts, strip malls, or studios,
a rabble of cars and pedestrians
outside, where a world of time
ticks through stoplights,
crosswalks, dinner hours.

The few men who join in
with baggy shorts and bony legs,
hopelessly stiff, foreheads creased,
lunge into downward dog or chair pose
or *dhanurasama*, submit to
the discipline mapped by the early sages,
yearning for liberated souls but taking
nothing for granted, surrounded by
women with miraculous flexibility
whose past lives have led them
to this nirvana.

# Bruja

La Paz is at its best on days like this.
The haze comes and goes.  I am always here,
my stall open to the air that wafts
down from cathedral spires.
My incense smolders, cutting through
the reek of market offal, and I wait
for needy ones to wind through corridors
of onions and rice to find me.

The part in my hair is perfect,
straight east to west when I sit
on this crate.  Deliberately,
the women come forward,
shoulders wrapped in ruanas,
on their heads black bowlers, tilted.
One says her refrigerator needs blessing.
Another is strapped for cash.
A bachelor wants help finding a wife.
This couple is infertile.  Two brothers
prepare for a journey to the ocean.
None of them can do without me.

I tell them Christ is not the full answer.
Consider Tio, who lives underground,
guarding the riches beneath my display
of herbs and amulets.  For him, each morning
I drench the earth in alcohol.
Here is a chiseled stone from deep,
deep in the Andes.  Place it in your house
if your marriage goes bad.

Stop at nothing.  Ispalla, the potato spirit,
deserves an offering.  Burn and bury
a llama fetus.  Sprinkle shredded coca
leaves on your floor.  No matter
that this cramped street
is indistinguishable from all others.
The power of the gods is available
even in the dust of markets.

# Biosphere 2

When food and water dwindle or abundance
overwhelms us we will snap the airtight lock
on this human terrarium.  Meanwhile--
the give and take of sun filtered
through bulging plastic, afternoons spent
tending plots of corn and a fragile stand
of wheat beyond the sleeping quarters.

It didn't begin this way.  At first
I traveled endlessly, a trip too desperate
to last.  Supplies gave out.  What more
could I do?  I recruited others:
a doctor, an agronomist, an expert in plastics,
an engineer, three more who understood
the double entendre of human culture.
We crawled into freedom, eight lives
converging, balanced by sex and task,
in a clear bubble on the desert.

Others visit at certain hours,
speak into the microphone, and await
our measured responses.  Seeing them
is not a problem.  Everyone gestures
abnormally.  The thick plastic is driven
outward by steady pressure: plant-fed air.
Leaning back-to-back against the membrane,
we begin to feel the heat of other bodies.

# Policeman

This week's shooting takes place in Odessa,
where the Times reporter calls the daylight "brazen."
Traffic stop, postal truck, civilians, a toddler,
lockdowns, shoppers fleeing a mall: phrases
borrowed from the last time or the time
before that. 8 dead and 25 injured.
After a while you run out of ammo
and words. One uninjured woman,
hyperventilating in her car, can't speak.
Another stammers, "We, we never thought
this, something like this, could happen here."
"Epi" means "upon." "Demo" means "the people."
"Epidemic" means "upon the people."

In downtown Odessa, an 8-foot tall
statue of a jackrabbit stands guard
not far from the Stonehenge replica
at the University. To the southwest,
meteor fragments are displayed at the crater.
In oil country, it's boom and bust.
Now a wind farm and a factory
producing weaponry for Army helicopters
provide jobs. This week's incident
is under investigation. No reported motive
for the shooter, who is killed by a policeman
with a sidearm pulled from a holster
strapped against the blue pants leg
that his wife ironed neatly in the morning
before he dressed, kissed her and left for work.

# Transients

By day they nod, ankles bare,
in the library reading room.
Magazines line the walls.
Papers lie before them
on mahogany tables.
Their eyes swell with cheap
drunks, cardboard nights,
the close smoke of cradled fire.

They arrive early,
bags and bedrolls tumbled
in their cracked hands.
Here neither purely for shelter
nor camaraderie, they sit alone
in worn plaid, shrugging in the heat.

The transients are grizzled
beyond learning, hacking
like miners. They take nothing
but wait for soothing night,
not long for this world,
charged with genius
and foundering in shadow.

THE WORK

# Logjam

Just this once, I say to myself
as I sit at my desk to write,
I will make a poem

that is not about poetry,
that has nothing to do
with the anguish of words

and how they glide submerged like otters,
though they must surface
for air eventually,

or how, like logs on a river,
they jam and tangle
until dynamite blows them free.

Yet I know, as you do,
shaking your head and smirking,
that my poem cannot escape

its poemness, nor the page its purpose,
any more than it can deny its origin
in the pulp of those logs.

Nor can the ink renounce the water
of its fluency even when it dries
and hardens into its dark promise.

# First Grade Teacher

Miss Duggar was
an old maid in sneakers
who rode a black bicycle
around town, groceries bagged
in her handlebar basket.

As she cruised downhill,
her gray hair flowed back
like smoke. This was the fifties,
and not everyone understood her,
but few doubted she could teach.

With her Brownie Instamatic,
she took black and whites
of us, posting them on the wall
with poems for us to copy:
"Look at Ken. Do that again."

She collected cigar boxes
and let us cut them up
with jig saws, our blocky hands
hacking out silhouettes
of camels and elephants.

We painted them, wearing canvas aprons.
She didn't care that we dripped reds
and blues all over the floor. Out of chaos,
she knew, came order--and the love
only amateurs bring to their art.

# Mrs. Perry

Wednesday after school I sit at the piano
trying to make up for another week
without practicing. My recalcitrant fingers,
like a bunch of dumb question marks,
work at the last minute
through my lesson in John Thompson's
Modern Course for the Piano.

When Mrs. Perry, regular as a metronome,
drives up in her old Chevy, I pray
that my natural genius will blossom
like a hothouse plant, but it never does.
I sweat and fidget on the bench
beside her broad hips, her flowered dress,
the faint scent of her deodorant.

Despite her grandmotherly bulk,
when she shows how it's done,
her fingers trip nimbly through the exercise
that plagued my lazy week. Everything
about her seems ponderous except those fingers.
I want her to go on playing right through
the book and into the next in the series.

I'd love to slide off the bench
and recline on the couch
sipping lemonade as she makes even
Franz Liszt, her favorite, sound easy,
a breeze. In the face of her fluency,
my little fingers are no more melodic
than a handful of stones cast over the keys.

When she makes my assignment,
gathers her books, and leaves
in her sputtering car,
I resolve that next Wednesday
I'll be ready for her. I'll toil through
thick and thin, black and white,
sharp and flat, major and minor.

As she rumbles off to another lesson,
I turn back to the baby grand, which crouches
like a giant toad in the living room.

# Coach

Birds die silently.
The day my Little League coach
launched a fly ball toward us
in practice, hitting a dove in flight,
we cheered until he ran
to cradle the feathers,
walk its death into the woods,
rest the bird beneath a tree.

Coach was a shelter,
a bag of nails, a way out.
We leave our bodies behind
when we rub the outstretched hand
of a marble statue, its fingers
glowing from burnished years.
Behind a door ajar wait
relics once belonging to us,
unremarkable as stones on a hillside
or a bird on the wing.

# Haircut

Barbers in my town wore ties
and white shirts, long-sleeved,
cuffs rolled like napkins.

Once Mr. Higgins draped
the sheet around me,
tucking it cleanly at my collar,

I was captive to his sleight of hand,
his wire-rimmed squint, emerald
visor billing from that bald head.

His wrists would flex and ripple
with the snap of scissors, artistry
of black comb.  Clippers,

whiny and shrill, showered
my hair onto waxed linoleum beneath
the sweep of pin-striped white.

The chair, chrome and lumpy vinyl,
creaked when he spun it
for a better view of crown or nape.

Tonic smells seeped into easy talk
that played over my young head
a rhythm of snip and shear.

And now, late in a good day,
I close my eyes and dream
of icy lather spreading like sea foam

on my neck and ears, the razor
only a moment away, straight
and narrow, honed and absolute.

## Day Shift

Facing a full moon
and clear sky
I drive to work
early, as the sun
creases the east,
and all the lights
down Main Street
turn green, as though
the town waited
all night for my arrival.
My transit on earth
frees the moon
to fade and start
its monthly collapse,
night now bereft
and under siege
by ruthless day.

# Microscope

My first birthday after our divorce
she sent me a microscope
from Ward's Natural Science.
It came in a wooden box
the color of her skin. The key
hung from a hinge like a locket
and opened the case with a click.

Inside, the door shelf held slides
and cover slips, miniature jars
in round niches. The single scope,
adjustable with a sturdy knob,
had a pleasing black sheen,
The thumb-sized electric bulb
tilted for the brightest angle.

As a biologist, she wanted me
to examine everything closely.
I devoted the rest of the day
to blades of grass, onion skin,
muddy water, a strand of hair.
I squinted, unable to find
the tiny footprint of a paramecium.

Then I married an astronomer,
a woman with her eyes on the skies.
When Mars was closer to earth
than ever, we rose at 4 a.m.,
set up the telescope
and peered down to see up.
Mars shimmered in our sights.

She noted the pin prick
of an ice cap, visible
on the planet's lower edge
and the dark threads of canals.
To my jittery eye, it looked as though
someone had shot a hole in the sky,
turned his back, and walked away.

# Bamboo

Today I cut down the stand of bamboo
behind the vet clinic.  Taller
than a two-story house, so thick
you couldn't fight your way into it,
the cane held a million starlings a night.
I dreamed it would ruin the neighborhood,
overtaking centipede lawns, flower beds,
and sidewalks. The flood of boney shoots
could sweep away dogs, jungle gyms,
chain link fences, and cars
like pebbles under a grassy glacier.

The vet clinic, situated on the verge
of rampant growth, suffered most.
The clatter of roosting birds
deranged the dogs, which howled all night.
Cats tore at their cages
when, at dusk, starlings poured
across the river, screeching black whorls,
before diving to shelter in the thicket.
Nightly the biblical horde drove us
to shotguns and whiskey.  Nothing worked.
The birds--the flocking birds--
sullied sundown in all seasons.

Finally, the canebrake had to go.
I hacked it down with a scythe and axe,
piled the spindly stalks,
and torched the lot of it.
All the grimy afternoon, smoke rose

and wheeled against the sky.
Tonight, I'm bone tired but can't sleep--
waiting, and listening.

# Gold Country

Time to rake aside the winter medicine
of oak leaf in the garden.
Beneath it all, the swollen earth.
Sunflower stalks rattle in the wind,
ten months after seed. Stones percolate
up through the ground. I lug them off,

then open the whole globe with my shovel.
I tuck in tomato plants,
expectant as ova. In shallow troughs
I sew zinnia seed. In the sanctuary
of July their red hues will rise
from clotted soil that reaches China.

While I plant I hear the chanteuse,
gravelly voice and sequins spangling
the composted air. Her song says
steal away at sundown, lean
the implements of culture against a tree,
and hasten to town.

Nature, said Heraclitus, likes to hide
herself. I could wash and wash
these soiled knuckles and still
they'd be my father's
with his country bearing.
Minutes away I drink in Sacramento.

Dark loam coats my boot heels.
In the Golden Acorn Tavern

a saxophone drains even the blood
of beets. The singer waits, toying
with glass beads, and gives
me the eye, alert for her next cue.

# Culture

Wayward in my compost pile, maggots
among potato peels and oak leaves bridge
the trough between my game of solitaire
and loam's unwieldy, earthbound violin
notes moaning in the garden's muddy lipstick,
garden-rich mid-morning at nine-thirty.

Radishes sprout in June.  I grew mine thirty
years back, well before I knew how maggots
swaddle death in gulps, transparent lipstick
on the mouth of summer, writhing bridge
to autumn's slow and mournful violin
of ripening pumpkins, pasture solitaires.

"Nothing will come of nothing," solitary
Lear intoned to quaint Cordelia, thirty
lines beyond her love, reluctant violin
already lost among the mewling maggots
in the palace.  No forked tongue could bridge
the painted words, as false as ochre lipstick.

King of my soil on the piedmont's lip, a tick
away from river bottom's solid air,
I dream of Lear's bedraggled heath and bridge
the centuries that yawn between us, thirty
decades wide and riddled with the maggots
hexing chords in nature's violin.

My daughter, pigtailed, held her violin
one day beneath these trees, wearing lipstick

red as autumn sweet gum leaves, ingots
glowing on the earth.  The solitaire
she played was lovely, fingers bridging
time to brazen Mozart, gone at thirty.

Now she hovers on the verge of thirty,
years beyond that yearning violin,
her limpid grace notes water under the bridge.
They drift past pilings, poised like tubes of lipstick
on her dresser, river solitaires,
so stark and sure, they'd baffle maggots.

I'll dwell with maggots, anything, to bridge
my solitude and that sweet violin,
bright as lipstick, glowing at nine-thirty.

# Bat in the House

The piano tuner came yesterday,
bent back every slipping note,
played parts of an overture from Bizet,
then shuffled off in his blind man's coat.

I'm washing dishes as a gray shape
cartwheels down.  Skimming the light,
it slices the air to bits, tiny cape
aflutter, or a misbegotten kite.

It swoops, clutches a bookshelf,
launches before I get a clean view.
I grab a Mason jar and brace myself,
ready to trap it and be through

with this intrusion.  The room wavers
like a sour note.  The bat just wheels
around the room, forward and reverse
no different as it peals

a strident sonar squeak, sounding
for an opening to the larger night.
The cat creeps in, sniffs what's pounding
the air, ducks a dive, and, uptight,

scoots out.  I wait for a sudden pause
on a wall, then clap down the jar.
Bat batters, wings crimped.  Tiny claws
scrape the glass.  Now, not far

to the back yard, where oak leaves fall
around me.  I fling him free.
Startled, he drops, a quick stall,
then torques up, airborne, three

quick beats and gone.  I slip
inside to build a fire.  Kneeling,
I fan a wing of flame, a rip
in the room's closed feeling.

Smoke the shade of bat fur makes a plume.
The upright gathers dust.  Night drains the room.

# Fruition

To morning's faint lantern,
you wake on the lip
of sheet and blanket
unsettled, surface
anew into wakefulness,
and recall the shallow
breath holding you
through dream and hunger.
You rise and carry
across noon light
the seed of evening
that swells over the hours,
bearing you back
into a harvest of slumber.

# One Mug at a Time

My goal is to turn, glaze, and fire
a quartet of matching mugs, a gift
for my wife. As I work on the first,
my thoughts slide to the next one
I'll make and then the next, until
the set is finished. Always taught
to plan ahead, I find this time,
the clay on the wheel won't center.
As it wobbles, I try to hollow it,
and soon only a wet heap remains,
spinning askew. I look to my teacher,
long black hair grazing her shoulders,
sleeves pulled up, who gestures
at my mess, grins, and says,
"Try building one mug at a time."
So I re-wedge the lump, just
as my mother kneaded bread dough,
and force myself to forget
about the matching set, turning instead
to my mother's supple hands coated
with flour, her wedding ring removed
and resting on the sill above the sink.
She and I together cradle the lump
as I work and this time shape
one mug with care, digging into the middle
only when it's centered, then slowly
coax a cylinder out of the slippery earth,
a single vessel unlike any other ever seen.

# Sawhorse

Less a horse than a stage
for my strivings,
this ungainly beam
with spraddled legs
takes my hammer's clout,
my chisel's carving
out of notches.
My saw bites through
an old dock plank
to bare rippled grain
in treated pine
like years of waves
that lapped while boats
banged and scarred
the edges but left
the inside new enough
for shore-bound life.
Water to water,
dust to sawdust,
this resurrection
levels my day
and muscles my hope.

# The Dream of Teaching

Each fall I know the dream will come.
The room gapes cavernous, bleak,
layered with September light.

The chalk board is scrubbed,
floor freshly oiled.
In front of the class,
tie much too tight, I grip
the desk as if straining
to lift it--or vault up
in a handstand.

My change, knife, keys,
and pocket watch
would clatter and bounce
on the bare desk.

I am locked in place.
If only I could see my hands,
utter one welcoming word,
the faces of my students
would emerge, books reappear
and bloom again.

# The Butterfly Tattoo

Minutes before class, as January rain
pelts my office window, she walks in,
sets down her book bag,
and slides off her motorcycle jacket,
letting it fall in a zippered clump.
Her spindle-thin arms, pale and faultless,
hang free in a skimpy summer top.
She pivots to show me the butterfly
tattooed on her left shoulder,
bright mandala in red and blue.
It's still sore, only two days old,
she says, craning around as if
to make sure it hasn't flown off.
It will follow her everywhere, wings
never lifting from the unfelt skin,
purple antennae drawn like tiny veins.
Some faded day she may wonder why
she drove across the state line one Saturday
to bare her shoulder for a stranger.
For now, my student smiles
with proud teeth, faintly painted lips.
I am as pleased as if she had written
the perfect poem.  As quickly
as I can glance down at my hands,
she has gathered her things and gone,
air trembling in her wake.

## The Student Poets

have it all figured out--how dreams
shatter, love goes awry, and even
daybreak brings a little sadness.

In their poems the beaches are sunny
with gently lapping waves, and mountains
rise like giants in the fluffy clouds.

But whatever the scenery, they know
the poet's consolation is only partial, lasting
no longer than the blink of an eye.

They know that a long thought needs a long line, while
a short one needs only a
word.

They understand the fine points of enjamb-
ment and how rhyme is for beginners,
infernal if not internal.

Their work flows from their pens
in a miracle of completeness. *It just came
to me*, they say, *late last night*.

I envy them that fluency, that ease
with the ways of the heart, that grasp
of life's daily disasters.

I have a lot to learn from them,
I, who can hardly write a line
without a lifetime of anguish.

## Volcano

The window goes dark,
and I study the film of dust
on my desk.  My lamp haloes
a word-strewn landfill, yonder side
of an oak plateau, flatter
than the unmade bed of clouds
around the lopsided pillow
of Mount St. Helens.
                              Dust settles
like sifted flour on the plain
where my elbows prop nightly.
Heat here builds like milk
in a cow's udder.  My wrists wring it
with effort, and milk soaks paper,
buttery phrases so far from where
I lived I don't know why
you need to hear about it.
                              Except that now
the vision of my mother's freckled hands
has entered the room, how late
at night she kneaded butter and flour,
humming beneath her breath
as I stood in the doorway, at the chasm
of sleep, never dreaming
as my father snored a floor above
that these scraps of regret
would erupt into the sky of this poem.

# Flare

Even after my last cigarette,
I pocketed matchbooks everywhere.
I could not forgo the magic flare
as a dark tip scored the gritty strip.

The tight combs of armless torsos,
helmeted soldiers huddled,
pleased me each time
I untucked the front.

I hated to tear one free,
breaking the symmetry
for sudden heat--
and light, love of light.

Matchbooks have vanished
from motel desks and bar counters,
giving way to Bic lighters and then
the demise of smoking itself.

We've lost the thrill of penciling
a phone number in the fold,
the trick of bending down a tab
to strike it one-handed, thumbing

a burst as quick and fleet as life itself.

# Drawing

Sheet of paper clamped to the board,
board tilted up to my ready pen,
pen the soul of my wavering hand,
hand revealing its partner in contour,
contour showing the lines of my palm,
palm poised to fold into gesture,
gesture becoming a slow dance,
dance a silent forgotten desire,
desire a sudden bloom of envy,
envy the force that urges my grasp,
grasp the garish light that melts,
melts the aftermath of struggle,
struggle the long obscure horizon,
horizon dark at the edge of day,
day the window that opens white,
white as the space at my fingertips.

# THE PATH

# Postcards

This shoebox packed with vistas
from souvenir shops and drugstores amasses
shots my camera couldn't manage, sights
missed in the rush to enter a museum
or catch a train. Riffling through them,
I speed from Independence Hall
to Miyajima's grand shrine to the guard
at Windsor Castle. Carl Sandburg's
study at Connemara Farm gives way
to the snowy grandeur of the Wasatch Range,
cave paintings, the Winged Victory,
then Churchill Downs, Siena's grand piazza,
and a hundred mismatched cathedrals.
One view of Bologna evokes the mozzarella
and eggplant soaked in olive oil that sustained us
one misty night. Another card brings a whiff
of wood smoke that filled the air in Aguas Calientes
as we boarded the dawn bus for Machu Picchu.
Then, I hear a mariachi band's midnight blare
in Arequipa where a jovial drunk urged us
to dance on the City Hall steps. The next day,
in the stunned silence of the convent
we entered at dawn, cobbled lanes
brimmed with prayers from a history
of nuns who found these dim portals
and winding passages world enough.

# Sanctuary

Bread blesses the aviary, picnic
of shadowy dawn. Familiar
horses crowd into the city.
Jack the Ripper is a ghost.

Gardenias of regret fester in a cloudy
landscape, party favors strewn behind.
All the red books rise into fellowship.
Wake to the booted minions.

Granted, the cathedral drives the pigeons
into ecstasy, the brute brick of comfort.
Spare the coin and custom. Embroider
your feathered name on the surplice.

Wait, wait, and the bell tower will sound
its blessing over the tiled roofs of the quarter.
Candles flicker in anticipation
of the sun's persistent cadence.

# Finding Mexico

*In general, Americans have not looked for Mexico in Mexico; they have looked for their obsessions, enthusiasms, phobias, hopes, interests--and these are what they have found.*
—Octavio Paz

I should have known my dreams
wouldn't surface in Juarez or Nogales
with their dusty streets, seedy bars,
strobe-lit strippers and cheap souvenirs.
Even the bullfight, panorama
of horn, cape, and sword
in Tijuana, ended badly, leaving me
little except the burden
of cheap wine in the sun.

I will seek out my obsessions
close to home--in the sweetgum shade
of my back yard or the rippling surface
of the pond down the street,
my enthusiasms in the cheekbones
and thighs of a strong woman,
my phobias in the abyss above
my head where constellations
of our latitude hang.

North of the border
I'll nurture hopes enough
to confine me for a lifetime.
In domestic dreams
I'll hear the rattle of Pancho Villa's
bandoleros, the sleepy strumming
of a guitar behind adobe walls,
the whispers of Cuernevaca,
Morelia, Oaxaca, Guadalahara.

# Machu Picchu

Arrive as dawn brightens
the abandoned fortress,
stones notched, knitted, locked.

Walk down abraded stairways,
and wind through alleys
that ghost the palms of the forgotten.

Pass through a gap in the far wall, and follow
the path along ledges, around boulders, chasm
on your left dropping steep to the valley

where a river winds like silver thread,
and a town sprawls near hot springs.
Hear the hum of the early *mercado*.

Climb the path up the peak that rises
like a bishop's miter. Find a niche
near the top and crawl through a passage

that opens onto the windswept pinnacle
where three travelers lie,
eyes shut against the sun.

Welcome the *caracara* that drops
out of the sky and perches at your side,
head cocked as though waiting for an answer.

Behind you, below, take in the maze
you wound through, gasping in thin air,
and wonder where you go from here.

# Olives

In late summer, Italian farmers stretch
nets beneath their olive trees to catch
the ripe fruit when it falls. When the mesh
bulges with the harvest, sagging only inches
above the ground, they tilt the olives
into bins and carry them away.
At first, the empty orange nets
ripple like a vast ocean beneath
a green canopy. Later, beginning to fill,
they look from a distance like hammocks
swaying with soldiers in dark heaps.

Or at least that is what I imagine
as I hike through the groves
early in the season when the nets
are still furled, giant cocoons
waiting to open. On just the right day,
say in late September, the farmers
must come and shake the trees
to fill the nets. Around noon
perhaps they sit in the shade
with bottles of red wine, cheese,
and round loaves of bread. Surely
they sample the crop, pronouncing
it delicious as they lounge and chat
in perfect Italian about the goodness
of life and the bounty of the earth.

The trail takes me over the crest
of a hill, and the Ligurian Sea
opens out below. In the sudden wake

of all that water, the olives become
a quaint memory. The stark sun
burns away the nets.
The farmers who toiled
to place them there drift into
the alleys of an ancient village.

## Laundry

Walking in Kensington,
I saw a young woman dragging
a bag of laundry down the street.
The London sun shone warmly.

She wore flip-flops and a black dress,
perhaps the only clean item
left in her closet.
She was straining at the bag,

so I offered to carry it,
and she was grateful.
As I shouldered her burden
I saw that she was beautiful.

Despite the heat, her skin showed
not the slightest sheen of sweat.
It seemed incredible
that she had any dirty clothes.

When I dropped the bag
at the laundry she hugged me.
Beneath the thin fiber of her dress,
she wore nothing.

## Good Friday

Enveloping us in overnight mail,
rain pours down in fat shadows.
A train whistles through the barricades.
We gamble with lanterns fashioned
from the daily news, printed precincts.

A woman with 60 cats blames the law
for her indolence. Reporters cradle
her complaints. The azaleas flame
gorgeously this year after a wet March.
Feast upon Easter candy.

Fat with old scandals, we ignore
the frivolous weather,
overcast candlepower, and carve
out a niche in the glowing sky.
Night descends like a mellow curtain.

We travel all day but return in time
for the evening report, litany
of burning statues. Lost artifacts
drift into Europe like gentle missiles.
In the end, we hammer out a cause.

# In Manila

*Religious cultists, convinced that flat tires were the key to salvation, deflated tires on scores of buses and cars Monday, paralyzing traffic throughout the city.*

—AP, 29 December 1992

They might have been clerks and shoppers,
strangers to one another, intent on lunch,
sifting through noon traffic.
When the first bus settled
to its wheel rims, the driver,
pulling away from the curb,
felt steel grind asphalt and only then
saw figures scurry to a parked Honda,
and on to a fleet of taxis, praying
over tires.  Whole intersections
filled with hissing, as air foul
from enclosure escaped to gather
in holy miasma above the rabble.
In an hour baffled policemen
handcuffed the peaceful miscreants,
dragging them away.

Some trace this fervor to the vision
of a dark Virgin in yesterday's clouds,
others to some pilgrim's nightmare
of a thousand tires, devil-driven.
Many tell of a voice in the ear
of Honora Dimagila, who uttered the command,
barely daring to breathe, and later explained,
"Air is from God.  This is the solution
to the crisis in our country."

If a forlorn and travel-weary God issued
such a test, that would explain the resignation
of Honora and her thirty followers.
Safely at home, Fernando Santos, deflated
while waiting for a light to turn,
ponders how quickly we're shaken
in our search for some simple Eden
where only the salt breeze
across the bay from Corregidor,
or the smell of warm bread, fills the air.

# Outpost

Let's be clear about this.
Even the permafrost
will melt someday, whether or not
you and your thousand maybes
are still around to sink
into the resulting swamp.
You've driven me to this pipeline
of lies in a jeep outfitted
for rough weather
but damn near out of fuel.

Jonah, you know, also claimed
he was a victim of circumstance,
just got in with the wrong crowd.
But he could have avoided
the nightmare of that sodden belly
if he had only listened.
Others have been here even longer
than you and have survived
with nothing more
than an extra blanket,
a case of whiskey,
and a plan for spring.

The bay unfreezes with tropical speed,
I hear. You tell me how the fractured
ice booms, how by midday the channel clears
and waves lap the shore within hours.
Tell me you can't imagine
the salmon jumping again,
their bodies feathering up    .
to catch the light
we didn't know was there.

# The Letters

—after Edward Hopper's *Hotel Room*

I too have been in such hotel rooms,
the unadorned walls, whatever
their original color, faded
to a muddy beige, the thin mattress
topped with a threadbare sheet,
a blanket bleak as the wall.
Here, the dark chest of drawers
and overstuffed chair glow dimly
in sunlight angling through
a window from the west.

The woman seated on the bed
at first appears nude, but then I see
the bustier around her slim torso,
the outline of her shadowed head
showing bobbed hair from the twenties.
I know the heat of an uncooled
room several floors up,
the slight relief of clothes shed
after walking miles of pavement
in summer humidity.

I can feel the letter sagging
in her grasp, the words now freed
from an envelope just opened
in a cramped enclosure,
high ceiling its only luxury.
Despite the vast distance
between us, she in the painter's

crux of sepia angles, I, lost
in my own cubicle of recollection,
I long to save her—and myself.

Even the half century separating us
cannot dim the words we each hold,
scrawled handwritten syllables
we force ourselves to read again
and again. I imagine her pulled
forward, years beyond her solitude,
while my unabashed longing,
my regrets, coax me back to a day
or week or month before the letter
comes into my wavering hands.

# National Geographic

Dark women cradle babies
or stir pots over open fires
on the Amazon or the Zambezi.
If the photographer happened by
on laundry day, the river laps
behind silhouetted forms
scrubbing clothes on rocks.

Oblivious to their hard-muscled wives
and beaded children,
the men squat and smile through teeth
filed and kola-stained.
Or they freeze, tendons poised
to thrust spears into water,

Somewhere among the huts,
modest fires, glimpses
of deep forest--frames snapped
from a village--a white man stands
unshaven, dressed in khaki.
He is the writer
whose text fills the gaps
between pictures.
Perhaps he is with the chief,
taking it all in, imagining
what he could say
about the women with full breasts,
the heat, the tropical smells
that swirl around him,
the long trail home, the dark,
dark eyes that never blink.

# Dry Season in Ghana

Rooster crow and pan rattle
startle us from sleep.  Smoke
rises from morning fires.
Soon women labor
to market, burdens
on heads, infants
bound to backs.

Early heat in our rooms curls
paper.  Even straw mats
warm to the touch.
Beneath our balcony
coastal trucks grind
into this tin-roof town.
The market's murmur
swarms at us, stifles.
Vultures wait.

Conversations we try
lapse into tangles
of questions over steam
from fish stews,
peppered by tall women.
Words between us run
together in the heat.
We know this cannot last.

Night again, and drums
pound through open windows.
Naked in bed

we sprinkle precious water
over one another
until desert breezes
send us thinly
into African sleep.

# Hard Bargain

Two head masks from West Africa,
helmets of rough wood,
hang on my study wall.
One, a long-snouted pig face,
stares out through drilled eyes.
The other, a bird crest,
points down in a frozen arc.
Each is hacked from a single chunk,
painted ochre and white.

On my desk are framed portraits
of my two daughters, who know
the story of the hard bargain
I struck in a crowded market,
how I wrapped the relics in goatskin,
lugging them from Mopti to Timbuktu.

But they don't know I hold back
more secrets than the fading photos
from that hot journey. I can't tell them
why these masks remain with me
after twenty years, why at times
my mouth gapes open like the pig's
in hunger, or why like a wooden bird
I long to fly.

## ABOUT THE AUTHOR

 KEN AUTREY lives in Auburn, Alabama, where he helps coordinate the Third Thursday Poetry Series. He earned degrees from Davidson College, Auburn University, and the University of South Carolina. He is an Emeritus Professor of English at Francis Marion University in South Carolina, where he taught poetry, creative nonfiction, and advanced composition. Previously, he served as a Peace Corps Volunteer in Ghana and taught at Tougaloo College in Mississippi. He spent one year as a visiting professor at Hiroshima University in Japan. Autrey's work has appeared in *Chattahoochee Review, Cimarron Review, Poetry Northwest, Southern Poetry Review, Texas Review* and many other journals. He has published four chapbooks: *Pilgrims* (Main Street Rag), *Rope Lesson* (Longleaf Press), *The Wake of the Year* (Solomon and George Press), and *Penelope in Repose* (Evening Street Press). A full-length collection, *Circulation*, was published by Dos Madres Press. He is married to Janne Debes. They have two daughters and six grandchildren.

Author photo by Janne Debes

# ACKNOWLEDGEMENTS

Thanks to editors of the following journals and collections in which some of these poems first appeared, sometimes with different titles or formats.

*Atlanta Review*: "Bruja"
*Birmingham Poetry Review*: "Volcano"
*Cairn*: "Imagining Iowa, January 1936"
*California Quarterly*: "Cutouts"
*Clackamas Literary Review*: "Sawhorse"
*The Devil's Millhopper*: "Voices at Mid-Cut"
*English Journal*: "The Student Poets"
*Hubbub*: "Gold Country"
*Lullwater Review*: "Bat in the House," "The Poet Moves to Chicago"
*Midwest Poetry Review*: "Bamboo"
*Onionhead*: "Saint Joan in the Garden"
*Poem*: "Grandfather," "Outpost"
*Poetpourri*: "The Poet Meets His Class in the Chemistry Lab"
*Portfolio*: "Barn on Sand Hill," "First Watch"
*Savannah Literary Journal*: "Resurrection"
*South Carolina Review*: "Altar"
*The Sun*: "Hard Bargain"
*Southern Quarterly*: "Good Friday"
*Texas Review*: "Dry Season in Ghana," "National Geographic"
*Yemassee*: "Olives"

"Barn on Sand Hill" appeared in *From the Green Horseshoe: Poems by James Dickey's Students* (University of South Carolina Press).

"Bruja," "Finding Mexico," "Gold Country," "Hard Bargain," "In Manila," "Laundry," "Logjam," "National Geographic,"

"Olives," "Outpost," and "Saint Joan in the Garden" appeared in the chapbook, *Pilgrims* (Main Street Rag).

"The Dream of Teaching" appeared in *Out of Unknown Hands: Writing by South Carolina Teachers*, edited by Libby Bernardin and Linda Kirszenbaum (R. L. Bryan Company).

"First Watch," "Imagining Iowa, January 1936," "Plumbers," "Voices at Mid-Cut," and "Volcano" appeared in the chapbook, *Rope Lesson* (Longleaf Press).

My deep appreciation to Robert and Elizabeth Murphy for their fine work at Dos Madres Press. Thanks to Wendy Cleveland, Hank Lazer, and Robert Parham for their support and for their own exemplary work. Above all, I'm everlastingly grateful to my loving wife Janne.

Other books by Ken Autrey
published by Dos Madres Press

Circulation (2023)


For the full Dos Madres Press catalog:
www.dosmadres.com

www.ingramcontent.com/pod-product-compliance
Lightning Source LLC
Chambersburg PA
CBHW030916140626
46545CB00017B/2417